Original title:
Enduring Love

Author: Paulina Pähkel

ISBN HARDBACK: 978-9916-89-457-6
ISBN PAPERBACK: 978-9916-89-458-3
ISBN EBOOK: 978-9916-89-459-0

The Canvas of Us

In colors bright, we paint the sky,
With each brushstroke, dreams soar high.
Together we weave a tapestry,
A masterpiece of you and me.

With laughter loud, our hearts align,
Every moment, a chance to shine.
Through storms and calm, we hold our ground,
In this canvas, love is found.

Voices in Harmony

In whispered tones, our hearts collide,
A melody that cannot hide.
In every note, our truths unfold,
A song of warmth, a tale retold.

With harmonies, we bridge the space,
Notes of longing, sweet embrace.
Together we sing, a timeless plea,
In the chorus of you and me.

Bonds of the Unseen

In the silence, our souls connect,
Invisible threads, we both protect.
A glance, a smile, a calming touch,
These subtle signs mean so much.

Through woven paths, we softly tread,
Guided by the words unsaid.
A bond that dreams are often spun,
In twilight's glow, we are as one.

Hearts Like Ancient Trees

With roots deep in rich, fertile ground,
Stalwart in storms, we stand profound.
Branches reach for skies anew,
In life's embrace, our love is true.

Through seasons change, we still endure,
In quiet strength, our hearts are pure.
Together swaying, a timeless dance,
In nature's arms, we find our chance.

A Dance Beyond Eons

In twilight's glow we sway,
The stars begin to play,
Our souls entwined in night,
We dance till morning light.

Time whispers in the dark,
Each heartbeat leaves a mark,
In shadows, we entrust,
A bond that turns to dust.

With every twirl we spin,
The universe within,
Our laughter fills the air,
A cosmic love affair.

Through ages we have roamed,
In places unknown, uncombed,
Yet here we find our grace,
In this vast, timeless space.

So let us dance, my dear,
With rhythm crystal clear,
For in this fleeting time,
Our spirits climb and climb.

Silent Vows

Beneath the moon's soft glow,
Where gentle breezes flow,
We whisper words unsaid,
In quiet hearts they spread.

Your eyes, a tranquil sea,
Reflect what's meant to be,
In silence promises form,
A shelter from the storm.

With every breath, a pledge,
Across the world's wide edge,
Hand in hand, we will stand,
Together, always planned.

In moments hushed and still,
We know just what we will,
Our souls, a perfect tune,
Beneath a silver moon.

No need for grand displays,
In subtle, modest ways,
Our love, a gentle song,
In silence, we belong.

Infinite Horizons

The sun dips low, the sky,
A canvas brushed on high,
Dreams stretch like the sea,
Expanding endlessly.

With every dawn we chase,
A new and open space,
Where hopes and wishes dwell,
In whispers, we can tell.

Together we will soar,
Beyond the ocean's roar,
Embracing what we find,
In flow, our hearts align.

Each sunset paints the day,
In colors bright and gay,
As shadows start to blend,
Our journey has no end.

So let's seek what's unknown,
With courage, love has grown,
Across these infinite skies,
Together, we will rise.

My Heart, Your Home

In every beat, I know,
My heart, your warmth bestows,
A shelter from the storm,
In you, I find my form.

With every whispered prayer,
Together, we both share,
This space where love resides,
A place where hope abides.

Through laughter, tears we weave,
A tapestry believe,
With colors bright and bold,
In stories yet untold.

So take my hand, my dear,
No worries, no more fear,
For in this life we roam,
My heart, it feels like home.

In every smile, I see,
The future we can be,
Together, side by side,
In love, we both confide.

When Stars Align

In the quiet of the night,
Whispers dance in silver light.
Hearts align with cosmic flare,
Dreams take flight in the still air.

Moments twinkling in the dark,
Each a beacon, each a spark.
Fates entwined, a woven thread,
In this magic, fears are shed.

Like constellations in the sky,
Promises float, they never die.
With open eyes, we see the signs,
Two souls meet when stars align.

Guided by an unseen hand,
Together, we will take a stand.
In the vastness, love's embrace,
A journey shared, a sacred space.

So let us soar through endless night,
Chasing dreams in moonbeam light.
For in this universe, so wide,
Our hearts forever will abide.

The Promise of Tomorrow

Each dawn brings a new refrain,
A gentle touch, a sweet refrain.
With golden rays that warm the day,
Hope renews in every way.

Through trials faced and shadows cast,
We hold on tight, we break no fast.
In every setback, lessons shine,
With courage built on love divine.

Beneath the weight of yesterday,
We lift our heads, we find the way.
For every end, there's a new start,
And in the journey lies the art.

We'll chase the sun, we'll feel its glow,
In every heartbeat, promise flows.
The future calls, we hear the sound,
A symphony that knows no bound.

With hands entwined, we'll face the fight,
Through darkest hours, we'll find the light.
The promise written in the skies,
Together, we shall rise and rise.

Unfading Echoes

In silent woods where shadows play,
Echoes linger, night meets day.
Softly whispering tales of old,
Stories woven, memories told.

Time may pass and seasons change,
Yet in the heart, love's never strange.
With every echo heard anew,
The strength of bonds will pull us through.

Reflections dance in moonlit streams,
Carrying forth our sweetest dreams.
In the stillness, voices sing,
Of warmth, of joy, of everything.

With every heartbeat, every sigh,
The past remains, it will not die.
In every corner, in every space,
Unfading echoes of our grace.

So let us cherish, let us hold,
The stories shared, the hearts so bold.
For in these echoes, we shall find,
A love eternal, intertwined.

Against the Ravages of Time

A fleeting moment slips away,
Like grains of sand in bright sun's ray.
Yet in the depths of every hour,
We find the strength, we bloom like flower.

With each tick of the clock's embrace,
We carve our names in time and space.
Through storms and trials, we stand fast,
Holding tight to what will last.

For every wrinkle tells a tale,
Of laughter shared and love's sweet sail.
Though age may come, it cannot steal,
The memories that hearts reveal.

Through fading light and shifting skies,
Resilience glows, it never dies.
Against the tide, we stand our ground,
In life's deep sea, our love is found.

So let us dance through days that fade,
With hands held tight, our fears allayed.
For time may pass, but we will fight,
To keep our flame, forever bright.

The Gold Amongst the Gray

In shadows thick the moment sways,
A glint of light cuts through the haze.
Amidst the dull, a spark remains,
The heart ignites, though hope restrains.

With every struggle, patience grows,
In muted times, a strength that flows.
When darkness looms and fears arise,
The gold appears, a bright surprise.

Through aching nights and endless days,
In sorrow's grip, the spirit plays.
Like whispers soft, the courage stays,
Through battles fought, we find our ways.

Beyond the gray, the sun breaks through,
For every tear, there's joy anew.
In life's vast maze, the dreams we chase,
The gold we seek, the love we embrace.

So hold the light, let shadows fade,
In every doubt, be unafraid.
For in the heart, where warmth can lay,
The gold will shine amidst the gray.

Through Every Trial

In storms of doubt, we stand our ground,
The strength within, in silence found.
With every step, the path unfolds,
A tale of courage, quietly told.

Through every trial, bonds we share,
In whispered hopes, in loving care.
When burdens weigh, and skies are grey,
Together strong, we find our way.

With hearts entwined, we face the night,
In darkest times, we seek the light.
Through struggles faced, our spirits rise,
A tapestry of endless skies.

In every tear, a lesson lies,
In every smile, a bright surprise.
With open minds, we learn to grow,
Through every trial, love’s seeds we sow.

So walk with me, side by side,
With faith in hearts, we'll abide.
For in this journey, hand in hand,
We find the strength to rise and stand.

Flows Like Water

Like rivers deep, our thoughts will flow,
In gentle curves, where moments glow.
Through every bend, the current guides,
The pulse of life, where truth abides.

It twists and turns, a dance so sweet,
In quiet pools, our shadows meet.
With every wave, a chance to learn,
In fluid grace, our passions burn.

The laughter sings, the memories land,
In flowing streams, on golden sand.
Through changing tides, we learn to steer,
In every drop, our dreams appear.

So let it wash, this ebb and sway,
In all that is, we find our way.
For life, like water, shapes the shore,
With every gust, we yearn for more.

Embrace the flow, the wild cascade,
In gentle whispers, fears invade.
For in the depths where currents plot,
We find true peace, in every thought.

A Love Song Replayed

In softest notes, our hearts align,
A melody shared, so sweet, divine.
With every chord, a story plays,
In tender sound, affection sways.

Through whispered dreams, the voices soar,
In quiet moments, we find the core.
With every beat, a pulse so true,
A love song sung, just me and you.

In gentle rhymes, our souls retell,
A timeless bond, an anchored swell.
In ebbing tides, where laughter reigns,
Together here, through joys and pains.

Each harmony, a bridge we cross,
In every verse, we find the gloss.
With hands entwined, in rhythm sway,
A love song played, come what may.

So let it ring, the notes we share,
In every laugh, in every care.
For in this song, our hearts replay,
The sweetest love that lights the way.

A Symphony of Togetherness

In the quiet night, we share a tune,
Under the soft glow of the crescent moon.
Every heartbeat echoes, radiant and bright,
Together we dance, embracing the light.

Moments like treasures, stitched into time,
With laughter and love in perfect rhyme.
Hand in hand, we weave our story,
A symphony sung in shared glory.

Through storms and calm, we stand so near,
With every challenge, our bond grows clear.
In whispers of joy, in shadows of fears,
Together we flourish, through all these years.

As seasons change and the world may sway,
Our hearts stand strong, come what may.
In the tapestry of life, threads intertwine,
A masterpiece born, forever divine.

In the embrace of unity, we find our way,
Each note a promise, each moment a stay.
In this grand orchestra, our spirits unite,
A symphony of love, radiant and bright.

The Heart's Refuge

In the still of dusk, I find my place,
A haven where time's gentle grace.
Whispers of solace fill the air,
In this heart's refuge, free from despair.

Here, shadows soften, worries unwind,
A warmth that wraps, so tender and kind.
Within these walls, my spirit feels whole,
In each quiet corner, I nurture my soul.

Memories linger, like petals in bloom,
Filling the space with a sweet perfume.
Echoes of laughter dance on the breeze,
In this sacred shelter, my heart finds ease.

With every heartbeat, a story unfolds,
Tales of joy and dreams yet untold.
In the embrace of peace, I gently drift,
The heart's refuge, a cherished gift.

As stars appear in the velvet sky,
I close my eyes and breathe a sigh.
In this calm sanctuary where I reside,
Forever my spirit and heart abide.

Eternal Whispers

In the twilight's hush, secrets call,
Whispers of love, enchanting us all.
Threads of connection weave through the night,
In silence, our souls take flight.

The moonlight glistens on the sea,
Carrying messages meant for thee.
In the dance of shadows, hear us sing,
Eternal whispers of everything.

Moments like stars in the endless skies,
Flickering softly, they never die.
Each glance exchanged, a silent vow,
In the stillness, the sacred now.

Through ages past and days to come,
In every heartbeat, we feel the hum.
Bound by the threads of fate's design,
Eternal whispers, forever entwined.

So let us cherish each fleeting breath,
For in these whispers, we conquer death.
In the tapestry of life's sweet song,
Eternal whispers, where we belong.

Embracing the Endless

In the vast expanse where dreams reside,
We wander together, side by side.
Through valleys deep and mountains high,
Embracing the endless, you and I.

With every sunrise, hope is reborn,
In the embrace of light, we’re never torn.
Hand in hand, we chase the dawn,
The journey’s bliss, forever drawn.

Through whispers of winds that softly sway,
Guiding our hearts along the way.
In the dance of time, we make our stand,
Embracing the endless, heart in hand.

With courage unyielding, we face the tide,
Through storms and calm, we will not hide.
The universe whispers, love is the key,
In this embrace, we are truly free.

So let us soar on wings of grace,
In this boundless world, we find our place.
Together we’ll journey, no end in sight,
Embracing the endless, a pure delight.

The Colors of Being Us

In the morning light we shine,
Each hue a story intertwined.
Through laughter blue and sorrow grey,
Together we dance, come what may.

With vibrant reds of passion's spark,
Emerald greens that light the dark.
Golden yellows in dreams we trust,
Painting the canvas of our must.

Every shade a piece of heart,
From differences, we won't depart.
Blending hues, our spirits rise,
In love's embrace, we will not disguise.

In twilight's glow, we find our place,
Reflecting life in warm embrace.
Together we weave through dusk and dawn,
In colors bright, forever drawn.

Through every storm, our palette stays,
In unity, we find our ways.
The colors of us, forever true,
A masterpiece in every view.

Infinite Paths

Upon the road where choices lie,
Under the vast and endless sky.
Each turn a new adventure calls,
With whispers soft that break down walls.

In the forest thick with dreams untold,
Paths diverge, some timid, some bold.
Footsteps echo as we tread,
On trails where hope and fear are wed.

Mountains high and valleys low,
In every step, we learn to grow.
Branches stretch towards the sun,
In the dance of life, we are one.

With every fork, a chance to choose,
Embrace the unknown, there's much to lose.
Yet in the heart, we feel the pull,
Infinite paths, forever full.

No road is wrong, no way is right,
Each journey glows with its own light.
Together we wander, hand in hand,
In the world, we boldly stand.

Gardens of the Heart

In quiet corners where we grow,
Tender blooms begin to show.
Roots entangled in love's embrace,
Gardens flourish in this space.

From seeds of hope, our trust takes flight,
With morning dew, we greet the light.
Petals soft and colors bright,
In gardens shared, we feel the right.

We tend the weeds with gentle hands,
Through storms we weather, where love stands.
Together in the sun's warm glow,
Nurturing all the dreams we sow.

Seasons change, yet still we tend,
In every bloom, love's message sends.
Harvest time brings joy anew,
In gardens green, our hearts stay true.

In every flower, a story hangs,
Of laughter shared and sweet refrains.
Gardens of the heart unfold,
A tapestry of life retold.

In the Bridge of Time

In the twilight, shadows blend,
Moments fleeting, round the bend.
Time a river, swift and wide,
In its currents, we abide.

Memories linger, tales unfold,
Whispers of the young and old.
With every heartbeat, time we chase,
In the bridge of love, we find our place.

Footsteps echo on the path we carve,
Every choice a life to serve.
Moments woven, strong and tight,
In the tapestry, dark and light.

Tomorrow calls, a song anew,
Yet in the past, we find what's true.
In every second, joys align,
Lost in the bridge of time, we shine.

As seasons change and years unfold,
Our stories rich, in hearts retold.
Through every dawn and fading night,
In the bridge of time, we take flight.

The Rhythm of Us

In the dance of night, we sway,
Hearts in sync, come what may.
With whispers soft, we find our beat,
In this moment, love feels sweet.

Every glance, every touch,
Each shared laugh means so much.
In the melody of our days,
We find hope in love's bright rays.

Through storms that shake the night,
Together, we chase the light.
With every step, a story spun,
Our life a song, forever begun.

In the silence, our souls speak,
In the chaos, it's love we seek.
With every pulse, dreams combine,
In the rhythm of us, we entwine.

As stars above begin to shine,
We hold hands, your heart in mine.
In this dance, we'll ever stay,
The rhythm of us guides the way.

Roots Below the Surface

Deep in soil, where secrets lie,
Roots intertwine, reaching high.
Through storms and drought, they hold tight,
Silent strength in the darkest night.

Beneath the ground, life is spun,
Whispers of love in the warmth of sun.
Each tendril seeks, each root finds,
A connection forged, as nature binds.

Though above, the world may shake,
Below, foundations never break.
In patience, growth takes its time,
Emerging green, beauty in its prime.

Through seasons' turn, the cycle flows,
In quiet grace, the garden grows.
What’s unseen nurtures what we see,
Roots below, ever strong and free.

Embrace the earth, the life it boasts,
In every heartbeat, it quietly hosts.
For roots below hold stories vast,
In nature's arms, we’re anchored, steadfast.

Moonlit Promises

Underneath the silver glow,
Hearts whisper secrets, soft and low.
In the quiet of a starlit night,
We weave together dreams in flight.

With every breath, a vow we make,
In the shimmering light, our hearts awake.
Promises painted on the sky,
A bond that time will never tie.

In the shadows, a dance begins,
With moonlit beams, our love, it spins.
Every moment, tender and true,
In the night, it's me and you.

As the tides rise and fall in tune,
We find our solace beneath the moon.
With hope aglow, our spirits blend,
In the night’s embrace, love won't end.

In the quiet, our spirits soar,
Within these promises, forevermore.
Hold my hand, let’s chase the light,
Together, we’ll shine through every night.

Changes Like the Seasons

In spring's embrace, new life unfolds,
Colors bright, warmth in the cold.
Petals dance in gentle breeze,
Hope renewed beneath the trees.

Summer's sun brings laughter true,
Days long bright, skies so blue.
With every moment, we chase our dreams,
Life flows on, bursting at the seams.

Autumn whispers, leaves will fall,
Golden hues, a softer call.
In this change, we find our grace,
Embracing time, love we embrace.

Winter wraps us in its chill,
With candlelight, our hearts we fill.
In the quiet, thoughts reflect,
Life's sweet changes, we connect.

Each season brings its cherished art,
A cycle spun, a beating heart.
In every shift, we learn to grow,
Like the seasons, love will flow.

In Every Lifetime

In every lifetime we seek,
The whispers of the past,
Moments that we have shared,
Echoes that forever last.

Through dreams we wander far,
To lands both wild and free,
With every step we take,
Our souls in harmony.

The stars above us shine,
Guiding us from the night,
We dance beneath their glow,
In love, we find our light.

Each heartbeat holds a tale,
Of laughter and of tears,
In every lifetime, we grow,
Together through the years.

So take my hand once more,
As we journey on this way,
Two souls bound by the ties,
That time cannot decay.

Journeys Yet to Come

With every dawn that breaks,
A new path calls our name,
We carry hopes and dreams,
In this wild, wondrous game.

Mountains loom in the distance,
Rivers rush with glee,
Every journey we embrace,
Shapes who we're meant to be.

The winds whisper secrets,
Of places yet untold,
In the heart of adventure,
We find our spirits bold.

Side by side we'll wander,
Through valleys rich with grace,
In every step we take,
Life becomes our space.

With dreams like constellations,
We'll forge a path so true,
For every journey taken,
Brings me closer to you.

A Testament of Togetherness

In laughter and in sorrow,
We've built a world that's ours,
Through trials we have weathered,
Like blooms beneath the stars.

Each moment spent together,
Is a thread that's tightly spun,
In the tapestry of life,
We shine brighter as one.

With hands entwined in friendship,
We face the storms with pride,
A testament unwavering,
With love that won't subside.

The echoes of our voices,
Ring true in every space,
In every heart that knows us,
We leave a gentle trace.

For in this shared commitment,
We've found a sacred space,
A testament of togetherness,
In every warm embrace.

Threads of Connection

In every soft connection,
A bond begins to weave,
Through laughter and through silence,
In moments we believe.

The ties that bind us closely,
Are threads of purest gold,
With each shared story told,
A tapestry unfolds.

Across the vast expanses,
Our spirits intertwine,
In understanding and in trust,
Each heartbeat feels divine.

Through challenges we gather,
In unity, we rise,
For every thread together,
Is stronger in the ties.

So let us cherish always,
These threads that hold us tight,
In every single heartbeat,
We merge into the light.

Timeless Embrace

In the glow of twilight's kiss,
We find a space of endless bliss.
With arms entwined, we dare to dream,
As moments weave a silver seam.

Through years that pass like whispered sighs,
Our love remains, it never dies.
In laughter shared, in tears that stream,
Together we are one, a team.

The seasons change, but we stand fast,
With heartbeats syncing, unsurpassed.
In every glance, a story told,
A timeless warmth against the cold.

Beneath the stars, our secrets lay,
Forever drawn, we trust and sway.
In gentle breaths, our spirits dance,
In love's embrace, we take a chance.

A tapestry of dreams we weave,
With threads of hope, we never leave.
In this embrace, we find our grace,
A world built on a warm embrace.

Whispered Promises

In the hush of night where shadows play,
We share our hopes, not far away.
With every word, a promise forms,
A bond that weathers every storm.

The moonlight bathes your gentle gaze,
With whispered vows that softly blaze.
Through trials faced with hands held tight,
Together we ignite the night.

When doubts may creep and shadows fall,
I’ll be your strength, you’ll be my all.
In the silence, love's gentle call,
Will guide us through, we’ll never stall.

These whispered dreams, they carry weight,
In every heartbeat, we create.
A world where love and courage meet,
In each embrace, our souls complete.

As dawn approaches, fear takes flight,
In whispered promises, we unite.
With every breath, a vow renewed,
In love’s own light, we are imbued.

Unfading Hearts

In the garden where memories bloom,
We gather light to chase the gloom.
With every petal falling free,
Our hearts forever, meant to be.

Through laughter shared and dreams we spin,
Together we'll find where love begins.
With open arms, we face the day,
Two souls entwined, come what may.

Though time may test, and winds may blow,
Our love endures, this I know.
In every season, we will stand,
With hearts of gold, and hands in hand.

The stars above guide us at night,
With every twinkle, pure delight.
In the depths of silence, joy imparts,
A melody born of unfading hearts.

As sunrises paint the sky anew,
I'll find my home, forever you.
In every beat, in every start,
Together we'll thrive, unfading hearts.

Bound by Stars

In the vast expanse of endless skies,
We dream of worlds where love never dies.
With stardust whispers, our souls take flight,
Bound together, hearts shining bright.

Amid the constellations we find our place,
In every twinkle, we trace each trace.
Through cosmic dance, we weave and spin,
A universe built from within.

The night unfolds with secrets to share,
In the stillness, we find the rare.
With every glance, a promise made,
In the tapestry of stars, we're laid.

Though time may wane and shadows pass,
Our love, a beacon, forever lasts.
In astral realms, we'll write our tale,
As guiding stars, we shall prevail.

So take my hand; together we'll roam,
In the endless night, we find our home.
With every heartbeat, the cosmos starts,
For we are truly, bound by stars.

Through Life’s Winding Roads

Along the path we tread each day,
Winding bends beneath our feet.
Curves that twist in bright display,
Secrets held in journeys fleet.

Moments dance in sunlight's glow,
Whispers float upon the breeze.
In the shadows, lessons grow,
Leading us to hearts at ease.

With each step, we rise and fall,
Mountains high and valleys low.
Echoes of our laughter call,
Guiding us where dreams may flow.

Fellow travelers, hand in hand,
Stories woven, rich and bold.
Together, we take a stand,
Facing all the tales untold.

Life’s a winding, wondrous ride,
Skies that change from blue to gray.
In our hearts, a shining guide,
We embrace each passing day.

The Canvas of Our Days

Brushstrokes on a vibrant page,
Colors blend, both bright and dim.
Life's a canvas, sounds engage,
Every moment, every whim.

Pinks and golds in morning light,
Whispers of the evening star.
Each hue tells of joy and fright,
Artistry that's truly ours.

Memories like shades and lines,
Sketch the stories we have known.
In each corner, hope entwines,
Painted dreams in shades we've grown.

Time, an artist, bold and wise,
Crafting tales with gentle hands.
In each brush, the past still lies,
While we shape the life that stands.

So let us paint, with hearts ablaze,
Every moment, wild and free.
Together, create the maze,
On the canvas, you and me.

Love Beyond Horizons

In the twilight, whispers soar,
Of a love that knows no bounds.
Across the seas, forevermore,
Hearts entwined in sacred sounds.

Stars may dim, yet still they shine,
In the distance, dreams take flight.
Through the storms, we boldly climb,
Finding strength in darkest night.

Every heartbeat sings a song,
Melodies of trust and grace.
In this dance, we both belong,
Together in our sacred space.

Beyond horizons, hand in hand,
Love's a journey, vast and wide.
With each step, we understand,
Faith will ever be our guide.

So let the world around us change,
For our love will never fade.
In every phase, it feels so strange,
Yet, forever, we have made.

Treasures of Yesterday

In the attic, dust and grace,
Whispers of a time gone by.
Memories in a warm embrace,
Haunting softly, like a sigh.

Photographs of smiles and tears,
Frozen moments on display.
Each a glimpse of love and fears,
Stories built in yesterday.

Timeless echoes softly call,
In the silence, laughter rings.
Treasures stacked in memories tall,
Life we lived in vibrant stings.

Feeling the weight of the past,
Each old trinket holds a tale.
Yet with love, our minds hold fast,
In our hearts, the memories sail.

So we gather, share a smile,
Cherishing what once was whole.
Treasures linger, just a while,
In the depths of every soul.

Through Storms and Sun

We walk the path, hand in hand,
Through darkest nights, across the land.
The storm may roar, the winds may wail,
But love's bright light will never pale.

With every dawn, the sun will rise,
Its golden rays paint clear blue skies.
Together strong, we'll face the fight,
Our hearts aglow, a beacon bright.

In shadows cast, our spirits soar,
With every step, we learn to explore.
The tempest's rage can shake our core,
Yet in each storm, we grow once more.

Through laughter shared and silent tears,
We weave a bond that conquers fears.
In every trial, we find our song,
Through storms and sun, we both belong.

So take my hand, don't let it go,
Through winding roads, through highs and lows.
With faith as our guiding star above,
We'll weather all, embraced by love.

Ever-Blooming Garden

In the heart of spring, blossoms swell,
Colors ablaze, where shadows dwell.
Petals open to the gentle breeze,
Nature's canvas, a sight to please.

Each flower tells a tale of grace,
In this lush and vibrant place.
With every drop of morning dew,
Life awakens, fresh and new.

Sunflowers turn to chase the light,
Embracing warmth from dawn till night.
Roses whisper secrets sweet,
In this garden, our hearts meet.

Seasons change, yet love remains,
Like roots entangled through the rains.
Through thorns and trials, we'll stand tall,
An ever-blooming garden for us all.

So tend the blooms with gentle care,
Cherish moments that we share.
In every petal, find your part,
This timeless bond within our heart.

Tides of Togetherness

The moonlit waves dance on the shore,
Whispers of love, we both adore.
With every tide, our hearts align,
In this ocean, you are mine.

Seas may rise, and storms may clash,
Yet our bond holds firm and fast.
Through rolling waves and shifting sand,
Together, we will make our stand.

In every splash, a memory made,
In sunlit dreams, our fears will fade.
Like shells collected on the beach,
Our love is close, forever within reach.

With every footprint left behind,
A story etched in heart and mind.
The tides may flow, but we will stay,
In each other's arms, we'll find our way.

So let the oceans sing our song,
In unity, we'll both belong.
Through every ebb and rise we see,
Together strong, just you and me.

The Echo of Your Heart

In quiet rooms where shadows lie,
I hear the whispers, love's soft sigh.
The echo of your heartbeat flows,
A rhythm that forever grows.

In every space, your laughter rings,
A melody the stillness brings.
With every breath, a tale unfolds,
In gentle tones, your love I've told.

Through distant nights and starry skies,
Your essence lingers, never dies.
A symphony of souls combined,
In every note, our hearts entwined.

With open arms, I hold you near,
In every glance, you draw me here.
The echo of your heart, so true,
A lasting promise, just me and you.

So let the world around us fade,
In every moment, love displayed.
Together, we'll face each new start,
Forever bound by the echo of your heart.

Whispers of Resilience

Amid the storm, we stand tall,
With strength inside, we will not fall.
The winds may howl, the skies may gray,
But through the pain, we find our way.

In shadows cast, we seek the light,
Our hearts ignite, a fierce delight.
With every step, we'll carry on,
In unity, our hope is strong.

When doubts creep in, we lift our heads,
Each whispered word, a path that spreads.
Together we rise, no fear can bind,
In whispers soft, our truths unwind.

The scars we bear, they make us wise,
A tapestry of lows and highs.
In every struggle, courage blooms,
From ashes fresh, new life consumes.

So let the world throw all its might,
We'll face it firm, we'll fight the fight.
In every heartbeat, strength we find,
Resilience flows, a bond so kind.

Heartbeats Across Ages

In every heart, a story dwells,
From ancient times, to current bells.
The echoes of the past still sing,
In every pulse, new life takes wing.

Through years we travel, side by side,
The laughter shared, no need to hide.
A melody of love resounds,
In every heartbeat, joy abounds.

From child to sage, we weave the thread,
With wisdom earned and tears we've shed.
Each moment lived, a timeless dance,
In memories held, we find our chance.

Across the ages, voices blend,
In whispered dreams, our spirits mend.
Together we'll traverse each phase,
With heartbeats strong, we’ll write our maze.

So let the clock tick on and trace,
The rhythm of our shared embrace.
In every heartbeat, life’s refrain,
A symphony of love remains.

The Richness of Shared Moments

In fleeting seconds, treasures lie,
A shared glance met beneath the sky.
Every laugh, a gift we hold,
In warm embraces, stories told.

The morning sun, a golden hue,
In coffee cups, our dreams renew.
With every word, we build our throne,
In quiet chats, we're never alone.

A sunset's glow, a painted scene,
In nature's art, our hearts serene.
With hands held tight, and smiles our guide,
In moments shared, our worlds collide.

Through chaos bright, and calm so sweet,
In every turn, our lives complete.
In simple joys, the richness gleams,
Through shared moments, we craft our dreams.

So let us hold these times so dear,
In every laugh, and every tear.
For in the now, our souls will soar,
In shared moments, we find much more.

Love's Untamed Landscape

In wild terrain, our spirits roam,
Each path we take leads us back home.
With rugged peaks and valleys deep,
In love's embrace, our hearts will leap.

The rivers rush with stories bold,
In currents strong, our dreams unfold.
With every thunder, passion calls,
In love's great storm, no courage stalls.

The horizon glows with fiery light,
In twilight's hush, we find our height.
With stars above, we chart our way,
In love's vast night, we choose to stay.

Through tempest winds, we learn to trust,
In every challenge, our love adjusts.
With roots so deep, we weather fate,
In untamed lands, we celebrate.

So let the wilderness be our guide,
With hearts unbound, we'll take the ride.
For in this landscape, wild and free,
Love's true essence will always be.

The Unwritten Book of Us

In pages blank, our story starts,
With promises inked in tender hearts.
Each chapter waits, our hands to guide,
As dreams unfold, with love as our pride.

The whispers echo, soft and true,
In every line, I'll find you too.
Together we'll write what time can't steal,
In words that only we can feel.

Through storms we'll dance, through skies so blue,
In every page, my heart finds you.
A tale of joy, a thread so fine,
In the unwritten book, you are truly mine.

We'll pen the moments, the laughter, the tears,
Each verse a treasure that conquers fears.
With hope as our ink, we'll fill every space,
In this unwritten book, our love finds grace.

Whispers Between Hearts

In the quiet night, our hearts confide,
A gentle touch, where secrets hide.
With whispered vows, we carve the night,
In silent dreams, our souls take flight.

Among the stars, our wishes twine,
In every heartbeat, your soul is mine.
Through softest sighs and tender looks,
We write our love in unwritten books.

The rustling leaves, our silent song,
In every moment, where we belong.
A symphony played on the strings of fate,
In whispers shared, we contemplate.

As dawn breaks clear, our bond renews,
In every sunrise, love's colors fuse.
With whispers soft, we seal our pact,
In the language of hearts, we stay intact.

In the Shadow of Forever

Beneath the moon, we find our way,
In shadows cast, we choose to stay.
Each breath we take, a sacred vow,
In the shadow of forever, here and now.

Through tempest shores, our spirits soar,
No matter the battles, we ask for more.
With hands entwined, we'll face the storm,
In the shadow of forever, we remain warm.

Time may fade, like whispers lost,
Yet in our hearts, we'll measure the cost.
In twilight's embrace, our dreams collide,
In the shadow of forever, love is our guide.

As stars align, the night is bright,
In our own world, we find the light.
With every heartbeat, our spirits weave,
In the shadow of forever, we believe.

A Symphony of Two Souls

In harmony, our hearts compose,
A melody sweet that gently flows.
With every note, our spirits dance,
In this symphony, we find our chance.

Through crescendos loud and whispers soft,
With every heartbeat, we lift aloft.
Two voices blend, a timeless song,
In this duet, we both belong.

The rhythm of love, a sweet embrace,
In every measure, we find our place.
From silence born, the music grows,
In the symphony, our passion glows.

As life's refrain plays on repeat,
We'll hold the melody, bittersweet.
Together we'll sing, through highs and lows,
In a symphony of two souls, love knows.

Heartstrings in Harmony

In twilight's embrace, shadows dance,
Soft whispers carry, a fleeting glance.
Notes of laughter weave through the air,
Binding our spirits in moments shared.

With every heartbeat, rhythms align,
Echoes of memories, tender, divine.
Through life's symphony, we find our part,
Composing a melody, fueled by the heart.

Though storms may gather, we stand so strong,
United in chords, where we belong.
Each struggle a note, each joy a refrain,
Together, we flourish through sorrow and pain.

In silence we listen, in stillness we know,
The music of love, in ebb and flow.
A harmony stitched with resilience and grace,
In the orchestra of life, we find our place.

Unbroken Threads

In woven moments, soft like a sigh,
Threads of connection that never die.
With every stitch, a story unfolds,
Rich with the warmth that love always holds.

Through laughter and tears, our fabric is spun,
Colors of joy ‘neath the glowing sun.
No fray, no tear can pull us apart,
The tapestry we share is a work of the heart.

As seasons change, so too shall we,
Adapting with grace, in unity free.
Bound by the past and dreams that shall come,
Together we stand, our hearts like a drum.

Each thread tells a tale of hope and love,
A binding force that weaves from above.
Eternal connections, we’re never bereft,
In the loom of existence, forever we’re left.

Ageless Affection

Like the gentle moon that lights the night,
Your love shines through, an unwavering light.
In every lifetime, our souls will meet,
A timeless embrace, so warm and sweet.

Through the hands of time, we gracefully flow,
Carving the paths where pure feelings grow.
Like a river that winds through valleys and hills,
Our hearts together, a rhythm that thrills.

Each wrinkle a story, each laugh a delight,
In the dance of our years, everything feels right.
With you by my side, the world feels so bright,
Our ageless affection, a beautiful sight.

In moments of silence, our spirits intertwine,
In the softest of gazes, eternal design.
Together we blossom, knowledge profound,
In the garden of time, our love knows no bound.

Through Every Season

In spring's gentle breath, new life awakens,
Petals unfurl, sweet joy overtaken.
With laughter and light, the days start to bloom,
Filling our hearts with sweet love's perfume.

Summer dances in, with warmth and delight,
Infinite sunsets, hearts shining bright.
Days spent in whispers, in soft, golden rays,
Creating memories that linger and blaze.

Autumn arrives with a canvas of gold,
Leaves drifting softly, our stories retold.
In the chill of the air, we find comfort near,
In each other's presence, we hold all that's dear.

As winter calls forth, its silence and peace,
In the quiet of snow, our worries release.
Wrapped in your warmth, like a blanket we tread,
Through every season, our love we'll be fed.

A Silk Road of Affection

In whispers soft, our journeys weave,
Threads of warmth, we gently cleave.
Through desert sands, our spirits soar,
Each heartbeat maps a hidden shore.

As caravans in twilight's grace,
We navigate this sacred space.
With every step, the world unfolds,
Our love, a tapestry of gold.

In twilight's glow, we find our way,
Amongst the stars, where dreamers play.
The silk that binds, a precious thread,
In every word, in all that's said.

Through ancient paths of light and shade,
We write the stories, love portrayed.
Each treasure shared, a silent vow,
In every moment, here and now.

In echoes soft of days gone by,
We trace the lines, the low and high.
This road of silk, where hearts intwine,
A map of love, forever mine.

The Light That Guides

In shadows deep, your smile shines bright,
A beacon strong, through darkest night.
With every step, you light the way,
A gentle glow that will not sway.

Through stormy seas and winding roads,
Your love, my guide, the compass codes.
When tempests roar, you're by my side,
Through every wave, we will not hide.

Your laughter dances like the dawn,
A symphony of hope, reborn.
In quiet moments, still and pure,
Your presence whispers, I am sure.

In times of doubt, you lift me high,
Your warmth, a sun in endless sky.
With every heartbeat, fate aligns,
In love's embrace, our star still shines.

Together in this timeless space,
With dreams that time can not erase.
We walk the path where shadows slide,
With you, my love, my light, my guide.

Curled in Time's Embrace

In twilight hours, we softly meet,
Curled in time, where hearts feel sweet.
With whispered dreams and soft caress,
In love's cocoon, we find our rest.

The clock may tick, but we won't haste,
In moments still, we taste the grace.
Each breath draws close, a sacred dance,
In time's embrace, we take our chance.

With every gaze, the world dissolves,
In silent truths, our story evolves.
The shadows fade, the light stands still,
Our love a force, a constant will.

In curls of warmth, we share our dreams,
In moonlit skies, the softest beams.
With you, the seconds stretch and bend,
In time's embrace, my love, my friend.

As seasons change, our hearts remain,
In echoes sweet, love's tender reign.
Together here, with souls aligned,
In timeless space, our hearts entwined.

A Love that is a Slow Burn

In embers low, our fire glows bright,
A steady flame, a warm delight.
With gentle hands, we stoke the heat,
In patience learned, our souls complete.

Through seasons change, the passion grows,
A dance of time, where love bestows.
With every glance, a spark ignites,
In whispered dreams, we reach new heights.

The world may rush, but we will savor,
Each moment shared, a sweet flavor.
In quiet nights and whispered tunes,
Our hearts align beneath the moons.

With softest words, we weave the night,
In tender touches, hearts take flight.
Each glance, a promise, warm and true,
A slow burn love, forever new.

In warmth we find the strength to grow,
A love that ebbs with gentle flow.
With every heartbeat, time transcends,
In slow burn's glow, our journey bends.

Hand in Hand Through Time

Through the years, we walk together,
Each step in sync, no need for tether.
Memories born of laughter and tears,
Our love endures, defying all fears.

In seasons of change, we stand as one,
Facing the storms, embracing the sun.
With every glance, a spark ignites,
Hand in hand, we chase the lights.

As time unfolds, our story grows,
With whispered dreams and shared echoes.
No moment lost, each heartbeat counts,
In this dance of life, love surmounts.

With every wrinkle, our beauty glows,
In silent support, our courage shows.
We treasure the past, yet seek the new,
Hand in hand, just me and you.

Forever entwined, through thick and thin,
In every loss, together we win.
Our tale is written not on a page,
But in the heart, through every age.

Resilient Bonds

Through trials faced and battles fought,
Our hearts connect, with lessons taught.
A bond like steel, both strong and true,
In every storm, I stand with you.

With laughter shared and tears embraced,
In every moment, love is placed.
A tether formed in the darkest night,
In each other's arms, we find our light.

Though paths may twist and turns may bend,
We rise together, hand in hand, my friend.
The roots run deep, through sorrow and cheer,
Our spirits soar, there's nothing to fear.

For in the silence, we share a song,
A melody where we both belong.
Resilient hearts, forever we grow,
Together we'll face whatever winds blow.

As seasons change, and time flows fast,
We'll hold each other in shadows cast.
A bond unbroken, a testament kind,
In every heartbeat, our souls aligned.

The Unwritten Chapters

In the book of life, our pages wait,
Blank but beckoning, to write our fate.
With every step, new tales will unfold,
Adventures await, bright and bold.

With ink of dreams, we'll pen our way,
Through dusk and dawn, come what may.
Each word a promise, each line a fight,
Together we'll dance in the morning light.

The chapters hold seasons, laughter, and tears,
Each whisper of hope, dissipating fears.
With every choice, our story rewrites,
In the tapestry of days and nights.

So take my hand, let's journey afar,
Through uncharted lands, beneath every star.
With courage ignited, our hearts interlace,
In the unwritten chapters, our dreams we'll chase.

The final line is yet to be penned,
With love as our guide, on this we depend.
As we write our story, I vow to be true,
For each chapter is love, just me and you.

Light in the Darkness

When shadows fall and fears arise,
You are my beacon, my bright skies.
In the silence where doubts may sigh,
Love's gentle glow will never die.

Through winding paths that seem unclear,
Your warmth surrounds, I have no fear.
With every heartbeat, hope takes flight,
A flame that dances, our guiding light.

In whispers soft, your voice I hear,
A melody that calms my fear.
Together we face the unknown night,
Hand in hand, we embrace the light.

With every struggle, together we thrive,
In the depth of darkness, our spirits alive.
For love's a lantern, forever it shines,
In the darkest hours, our fate aligns.

And when the dawn breaks bright and clear,
I'll hold you close, wipe every tear.
For through the trials, we have learned,
In love's true light, our souls are burned.

Forever in This Moment

In the stillness of the night,
Whispers dance, taking flight.
Hearts entwined, a gentle sway,
We're lost in time, come what may.

Each breath, a promise we share,
Dreams unfurling, light as air.
Here and now, a sacred place,
Forever etched, your warm embrace.

Time stands still, a fleeting kiss,
In this moment, eternal bliss.
No shadows creep, no fears to face,
Just the magic of our grace.

Stars above, a silent guide,
In this dance, we won't divide.
With every heartbeat, love ignites,
Together bound, we chase the nights.

So let us linger, hold on tight,
In forever's glow, purest light.
For in this moment, we are free,
You and I, our destiny.

Threads of Destiny

Woven tightly, a tapestry,
Every thread, a mystery.
Paths entwined, our fates align,
In this dance, your hand in mine.

Each twist unveils a brand-new tale,
With every heartbeat, we set sail.
Threads of gold, threads of fate,
Binding souls as we await.

Moments precious, stitched with care,
In the fabric, love lays bare.
Dreams reflected in the weave,
In this journey, we believe.

Every folly, every tear,
Strengthens bonds, our hearts adhere.
Infinite patterns, life's design,
With every step, your path aligns.

Together we will forge the way,
Through the night into the day.
Hand in hand, against the storm,
In our threads, forever warm.

Seasons of Affection

Springtime blooms in your laughter,
Sunshine drapes, a warm embrace.
Summer nights, heartbeats faster,
In each moment, we find grace.

Autumn leaves in shades of gold,
Whispers carried on the breeze.
Memories cherished, stories told,
In this dance, our hearts find ease.

Winter's chill brings us close,
Fireside chats, soft and bright.
In the silence, love's sweet prose,
Warmth ignited by soft light.

Through every season, hand in hand,
Together we will walk the land.
Weathering storms and blue skies clear,
In this cycle, love draws near.

With every turn, we find our way,
In seasons' dance, come what may.
Eternal bloom, our hearts will know,
In every moment, love will grow.

Beneath the Same Sky

Underneath this vast expanse,
Stars awaken, join our dance.
Clouds drift by, a gentle sigh,
Together dreaming, you and I.

Moonlit nights and sunsets bright,
In the stillness, hearts take flight.
Whispers shared, in the soft glow,
Beneath the sky, our spirits flow.

Every heartbeat, a longing true,
Guided by the love we pursue.
Distance fades, a fleeting thought,
In this moment, time is caught.

Through laughter, tears, we journey on,
Hand in hand until the dawn.
The same sky binds us, near or far,
In its embrace, there you are.

So let us cherish what we find,
Under skies, our souls aligned.
With every star, we'll leave a trace,
Beneath the same sky, love's embrace.

The Depths of Your Gaze

In the shadows, secrets lie,
A world unfolded in your eye.
Whispers soft, a silent plea,
The depths reveal what we can't see.

Moments linger, time stands still,
A tranquil heart, a quiet thrill.
You pull me close, I lose my way,
In the depths of your gaze, I stay.

Each glance a spark, a tender fire,
Igniting dreams, deepening desire.
A gaze that shifts, yet holds me tight,
In your eyes, I find my light.

An ocean wide, yet oh so near,
The silent thoughts, the unvoiced fear.
With every look, the world does fade,
In the depths of your gaze, I wade.

As twilight falls and shadows creep,
In your embrace, my heart will leap.
I dive and drown, yet feel so free,
The depths of your gaze call out to me.

A Starlit Promise

Underneath the velvet night,
Whispers weave in silver light.
Every star a vow unbroken,
A starlit promise softly spoken.

The moon above, our silent guide,
In its glow, our dreams confide.
Fingers trace the paths we make,
In starry realms, our hearts awake.

Each twinkle sings a tale of old,
Adventures new, and glories bold.
In this dance, we find our way,
As stars align, come what may.

Together here, hand in hand,
In the vastness, we take a stand.
With every wish upon the skies,
A starlit promise never dies.

As dawn approaches, shadows blend,
Yet in our hearts, we will defend.
Underneath the morning's haze,
The starlit promise brightly stays.

Nightfall and Morning Light

When nightfall drapes the world in peace,
The stars awake, the chaos cease.
In whispered dreams, our spirits fly,
Night's gentle arms, a lullaby.

Moonlit paths of silver gleam,
In shadows cast, we weave a dream.
Each heartbeat echoes soft and low,
Embracing all the night can show.

Yet with each dawn, the light must break,
To shatter silence, a new awake.
Morning light peeks through the trees,
Breathe in deep, let worries please.

In the dance of dusk and dawn,
We find our strength, we carry on.
Through night’s embrace, to morning’s ray,
Life’s precious moments softly sway.

With every cycle, love remains,
In nightfall’s hush and morning's gains.
Together here, steadfast and bright,
We cherish both the dark and light.

Unwavering Waves

Along the shore where silence breathes,
The ocean hums beneath the leaves.
Unwavering waves rise and fall,
Each whispering tide, a timeless call.

In the moon’s glow, reflections dance,
A serenade, a fleeting chance.
Every crest a story spun,
Of journeys past and battles won.

With every crash, the world unwinds,
The heart echoes what it finds.
In salty air, we seek to be,
As waves embrace both you and me.

Together strong, we ride the storm,
In every surge, our hearts grow warm.
Though tides may shift and shores may fade,
Unwavering waves, the bond we've made.

When sunlight breaks and colors blaze,
The ocean's song, a fervent praise.
In harmony, our spirits rise,
Unwavering love beneath the skies.

The Dance of Us

In twilight's embrace, we sway,
Lost in the rhythm, come what may.
Your hand in mine, a perfect fit,
With every heartbeat, we commit.

The stars above, they shine so bright,
Guiding our souls through this sweet night.
With every turn, our shadows blend,
In this moment, time has no end.

The world fades out, it's just us two,
In the dance of life, we find what's true.
Each step a promise, each laugh a sigh,
Together we soar, like birds on high.

The music calls, it lifts us high,
In perfect harmony, we never die.
With whispered dreams, we take our flight,
In the dance of us, we find our light.

So let the night, embrace the thrill,
In every sparkle, our hearts will fill.
With memories woven, side by side,
In this sweet dance, we will abide.

Shared Breath of Eternity

In quiet woods, where whispers dwell,
Two hearts beat on, they know it well.
A shared breath, a fleeting glance,
In the moment, love’s sweet chance.

As shadows stretch, the twilight calls,
With every echo, our love enthralls.
Time slips by, yet we remain,
In shared silence, never in vain.

From dawn's blush to evening's glow,
Our story weaves, as rivers flow.
With every sigh, our spirits blend,
A journey long, with no end.

We paint the skies with colors bright,
In the tapestry of day and night.
Each memory, a thread we weave,
In shared breath, we truly believe.

So let us breathe, in rhythms sweet,
In every heartbeat, we’re complete.
Together forever, hearts in tune,
In the dance of life, we meet the moon.

Together Through Time

In ancient fields, where ages blend,
With every heartbeat, we transcend.
Gathered moments, both old and new,
Together through time, me and you.

The sands flow fast, yet we hold tight,
In every dusk, we find our light.
With laughter shared and tears we've cried,
In pockets of time, we ever bide.

The seasons change, yet love won't fade,
In every shadow, memories laid.
Through storms we've walked, hand in hand,
Together we rise, a perfect band.

The clock may tick, but we are free,
In every glance, eternity.
Through every challenge, we renew,
With whispers soft, our love rings true.

So take my hand, let's seize the day,
In every moment, come what may.
Together we dance, with love as our rhyme,
In the timeless beauty, we'll always climb.

Unraveling the Threads

In the loom of life, threads intertwine,
With each passing day, your heart is mine.
Unraveling stories, stitched from the past,
In patterns of joy, our love will last.

With gentle hands, we weave our tale,
Through laughter loud and whispers frail.
In the fabric of fate, we find our way,
Each thread a memory, come what may.

The colors bright, they dance and play,
In the tapestry of us, night and day.
With every stitch, our dreams take flight,
Unraveling hopes, in shared delight.

Through storms and sun, the threads may fray,
But in our love, they'll find their way.
Together we mend, with nimble grace,
In the quilt of life, we find our place.

So let's embrace this woven view,
In the art of living, just us two.
In every thread, our story's spun,
Unraveling love, when all is won.

In the Soft Embrace of Time

A whisper floats on gentle air,
Moments glimmer, sweet and rare.
Each tick a tale, each tock a sigh,
In time's embrace, we drift and fly.

Echoes dance in twilight's glow,
Memories weave, a soft tableau.
Silent shadows, soft as dreams,
In time's embrace, all silence screams.

The passing hours, like grains of sand,
Fleeting moments, hand in hand.
We hold on tight, afraid to part,
Yet time unveils the beating heart.

A symphony of days goes by,
In each goodbye, a lingering sigh.
Yet in the stillness, love will bind,
Forever etched in heart and mind.

The Tapestry of Us

Threads of laughter, strands of care,
Woven together, moments rare.
Each color bright, each pattern true,
In the tapestry, it's me and you.

Stitched with dreams, adorned with grace,
Every stitch tells of our place.
In storms we've weathered, joy we've known,
We weave our love, a world grown.

Fingers intertwined, hearts align,
In this fabric, your heart is mine.
The beauty lies in every scar,
In the tapestry, we've come so far.

A legacy, with love conveyed,
In every hue, our hearts displayed.
Together forever, we'll always be,
In this tapestry, just you and me.

Seasons of Unfaltering Flame

Through winter's chill and summer's heat,
Our love endures, steadfast and sweet.
In autumn's dance, leaves spiral down,
In spring's embrace, we wear our crown.

Flames flicker bright in the darkest night,
Together we rise, fueled by light.
Each season shifts, but our bond stays strong,
In the heart's garden, we belong.

Flowers bloom as shadows wane,
Through every joy, through every pain.
We weather storms, we bask in sun,
In the seasons, we are one.

Time may change, yet love remains,
Through fleeting days and whispering rains.
In everchanging skies, we keep our aim,
Forever bound, unfaltering flame.

In the Garden of Forever

Where dreams take root and laughter grows,
In the garden of life, love gently flows.
Petals soft, colors bright,
In the garden, we find our light.

Moments bloom like flowers rare,
In whispers sweet, we fade all care.
Each heartbeat nurtures, every sigh,
In the garden, we learn to fly.

Seasons change, yet here we stand,
Hand in hand, across the land.
With every challenge, love reveals,
In the garden, our heart heals.

Harvests gathered, memories sown,
In the bloom of love, we have grown.
For in this space, forever's gleam,
In the garden of forever, we dream.

Beneath the Same Sky

Underneath the vast expanse,
Stars twinkle with fervent chance.
Whispers of night, secrets to share,
Beneath this sky, we breathe the air.

Clouds drift softly, dreams in tow,
Moonlight bathes the world in glow.
In every heartbeat, time stands still,
Together, we weave hope at will.

Winds carry tales from far away,
Guiding us through night and day.
Hand in hand, we walk this line,
Beneath the same sky, our spirits shine.

Seasons change, yet love remains,
In the silence, beauty gains.
Across the heavens, we find our way,
Beneath the same sky, come what may.

And when the dawn breaks, painting dreams,
Sunrise whispers, lighting streams.
In every hue, a promise lies,
Together forever, beneath the skies.

The Echoes of Our Laughter

In the garden, laughter rings,
Echoes dance on joyful wings.
Every chuckle, every cheer,
Moments cherished, always near.

Beneath the trees, shadows play,
Sunlight filters, bright as day.
We carve our names in bark so old,
Stories shared, memories bold.

Raindrops tap on window panes,
We find joy through little pains.
With every giggle, tears will fade,
In our hearts, a love cascade.

Time spins round, but we hold fast,
Each memory becomes a cast.
In the echoes of what we share,
Laughter lingers, everywhere.

And as the seasons come and go,
Our laughter adds a vibrant flow.
In the quiet, still we find,
The echoes of our love entwined.

Frames of Forever

In a snapshot, life reveals,
Moments captured, time conceals.
Frames of memories, side by side,
Each glance reflects a gentle tide.

Golden sunsets, soft and sweet,
Photographs where shadows meet.
Every smile, every tear,
In these frames, we hold you near.

Through the lens, our stories blend,
Every corner, love transcends.
Faded colors, vibrant hues,
In each frame, a cherished muse.

As years slip by and seasons change,
We find beauty in the strange.
Captured lives in frames of light,
Forever cherished, pure delight.

With each photo, time stands still,
In our hearts, a sacred thrill.
Frames of forever, hand in hand,
Together, we will forever stand.

Every Beat a Memory

Each heartbeat whispers your name,
In this dance, we're never the same.
Every pulse, a story told,
In the rhythm, love unfolds.

Moments flicker, flash like fire,
In our hearts, an endless choir.
Every beat, a memory dear,
In this symphony, you're always near.

Through the silence, echoes play,
In each breath, we find our way.
Tangled souls, forever we sway,
Every beat, come what may.

And as the stars begin to glow,
We dance to life's soft ebb and flow.
In our hearts, a timeless creed,
Every beat, a cherished seed.

With every dawn, anew we rise,
In your gaze, I see the skies.
Every heartbeat, pure and free,
In this love, we find our key.

Reverberations of Devotion

In whispered winds, your name I call,
A tender echo, I feel it all.
Through time and space, our hearts entwined,
A bond unbroken, love defined.

With every heartbeat, I find my way,
Guided by light, not led astray.
In shadows deep, your spirit glows,
A promise kept, forever flows.

The world may change, but here we stand,
In unity, we take our hand.
A symphony of souls so bright,
Together we dance, through day and night.

In quiet moments, your laughter rings,
A sacred joy that only love brings.
We navigate the storms with grace,
With every trial, we find our place.

From distant shores, I hear your tune,
A melody beneath the moon.
In every challenge, our love will grow,
In every heartbeat, a truth we know.

Love That Knows No Bounds

Across the heavens, our love soars high,
In galaxies, where we touch the sky.
A timeless bond, no distance can break,
In every moment, every choice we make.

Through valleys low and mountains steep,
In whispered dreams, our secrets keep.
We intertwine like roots of trees,
In gentle breezes and summer's ease.

Our laughter rings, a sweet refrain,
In joy and sorrow, love won't wane.
Through every passage, we carve our lane,
In hearts united, we'll feel no pain.

With every sunset, a promise sworn,
In every dawn, our love reborn.
No measure holds what we have found,
In every heartbeat, love knows no bounds.

Together forever, our spirits dance,
In every glance, a timeless chance.
Through fields of dreams, hand in hand,
In the tapestry of life, we stand.

Anchored in Forever

In every storm, you are my calm,
Your voice a soothing, gentle balm.
With roots in truth, we grow so strong,
Two souls in harmony, where we belong.

Through life's tempests, we navigate,
Anchored in trust, we won't abate.
In moments lost, we find our way,
A beacon bright, we won't stray.

The sands of time may shift and swirl,
But in your eyes, I see the world.
Through every challenge, I'll stand tall,
In love’s embrace, we’ll never fall.

A tapestry woven with threads so fine,
In every stitch, our lives align.
Together we face the ebb and flow,
In every heartbeat, our love will grow.

In the quiet hours, our dreams take flight,
With you beside me, my heart feels right.
Anchored in forever, come what may,
In your embrace, forever I’ll stay.

Firelight of the Soul

In twilight's glow, we gather near,
The firelight flickers, love sincere.
Within its warmth, our spirits blend,
A radiant glow that will not end.

Through whispers soft, we share our dreams,
In dancing shadows, love redeems.
The embers spark, igniting trust,
In every moment, it’s love we must.

With every flicker, our hearts ignite,
In the stillness, our souls take flight.
The flame of passion, forever bright,
Guides us through the darkest night.

Through trials faced, our fire burns,
In every lesson, the heart learns.
Together we brave the winds that blow,
In love's embrace, we’ll always glow.

With firelight’s glow, our spirits soar,
In every heartbeat, we ask for more.
Bound by desires that never fade,
In the warmth of love, we are remade.

Flames That Never Die

In the heart of the night, sparks arise,
Glowing embers dance, painting the skies.
Whispers of warmth in the chilly air,
A radiant glow, igniting our care.

Through trials and storms, they flicker bright,
A testament strong, a beacon of light.
Memories linger in the crackling sound,
In shared moments, our souls are unbound.

The fire of passion, it never fades,
Each memory cherished, no need for parades.
In the silence of dusk, we share our dreams,
Held together, or so it seems.

With every heartbeat, the flames grow tall,
In the tapestry of life, we weave our call.
From ashes we rise, with hope in our eyes,
Together forever, beneath endless skies.

So let the world turn and seasons change,
Our love, a warmth that feels so strange.
In the depths of the dark, our fire defies,
Together we stand, where true love lies.

Anchored Souls

In the vast ocean, we find our peace,
With tides that echo, and waves that cease.
Our hearts entwined, like ships in the night,
Anchored together, holding on tight.

Beneath the stars, we whisper our dreams,
As the moonlight dances on silver streams.
Through tempests and calm, we steadfast remain,
In the embrace of love, we share our gain.

Life's currents may shift, but we won't drift,
In every moment, we find our gift.
Through high and low, we navigate time,
Hand in hand, our souls will climb.

With every sunrise, hope glimmers anew,
In the depths of still waters, love shines through.
Through storms we have weathered, we still stand tall,
Anchored in faith, we'll never fall.

So let the wind blow, we will not part,
For you are the anchor of my heart.
Together we'll sail, charting our course,
In the ocean of life, love's gentle force.

In the Shadow of Forever

Beneath the stars, we linger so close,
In the shadow of dreams, where love only grows.
Whispers of time dance through the night,
In each other's gaze, everything feels right.

Moments suspended, hearts intertwined,
In the quiet embrace, our souls aligned.
With the warmth of your touch, I'm never alone,
In the shadow of forever, our love has grown.

Each heartbeat echoes a promise made,
In the twilight's glow, fears start to fade.
With the passing of hours, we bravely reside,
In the silence, our hopes become our guide.

Through the seasons of life, we will stand strong,
Writing our story, where we belong.
In the shadow's embrace, we find a way,
To cherish each moment, day after day.

So here we shall dwell, in love's gentle light,
As stars bear witness to our endless flight.
In the shadow of forever, we'll always stay,
In a timeless dance, come what may.

Echoes of Our Laughter

In the quiet of night, laughter still gleams,
Echoes of joy weave through our dreams.
In memories woven from days long past,
The light in our hearts, forever will last.

Through sunlit mornings, we chase delight,
In shared conversations that feel so right.
Each giggle and whisper, a reminder sweet,
Life's vibrant tapestry, isn't complete.

As seasons change, our laughter will ring,
In harmony's embrace, it's love that we bring.
With every shared glance, the warmth that flows,
In the garden of friendship, our spirit grows.

Through trials we've weathered, our bond only thrives,
In the laughter we share, our memory survives.
With each joyful moment, a treasure revealed,
In the echoes of laughter, our hearts are healed.

So let us remember, as time marches on,
The joy that we found, and the love that we've drawn.
In the echoes of laughter, there's magic anew,
Together forever, just me and you.

The Language of Glances

In the stillness, eyes collide,
Words unspoken, secrets hide.
A fleeting moment, hearts ignite,
In every glance, there burns a light.

Silent tales within a stare,
Every look, a whispered dare.
Mapping dreams with each blink,
In the silence, souls connect and sync.

With just a gaze, worlds align,
Two spirits dance, almost divine.
Where languages fail, feelings flow,
Through the eyes, true love will grow.

A fleeting touch that lingers long,
In a glance, the heart's a song.
From look to look, a story told,
In silent worlds, love's beauty unfolds.

Every glance, a tender kiss,
In the eyes, a boundless bliss.
Here in silence, we both find,
The language of glances, unconfined.

When Time Stands Still

In the quiet, moments freeze,
Time takes pause, a gentle breeze.
A heartbeat shared, the world fades,
Intimate dreams in soft charades.

A glance exchanged, eternity waits,
In this realm, love celebrates.
No ticking clocks, no rush to flee,
In your arms, time’s mystery.

Together bound, seconds glide,
In tender moments, we confide.
Every sigh lingers like a note,
In this stillness, we both float.

The seconds stretch like woven threads,
In whispered tales, the heart treads.
Wrapped in silence, dreams take flight,
Here in twilight, all feels right.

Lost in this enchanting spell,
Where love's echoes softly dwell.
In the stillness, we remain,
When time stands still, love's refrain.

Shadows Cast by Love

In the twilight, shadows play,
Dancing softly, night meets day.
Whispers linger, secrets told,
In their warmth, hearts turn to gold.

Hand in hand, we walk this path,
Counting moments, embracing laughs.
Every shadow, a tale to share,
In their depth, a love affair.

Beneath the moon, soft light beams,
Illuminating whispered dreams.
In each shadow lies a spark,
Guiding us through the deep dark.

Like silhouettes in moonlit glow,
Our love dances, gentle and slow.
Every kiss, a soft caress,
In shadows, we find our excess.

With every turn, love's echo stirs,
In shadows cast, the heart concurs.
Together finding our own song,
In the dark, we both belong.

Intertwined Journeys

Two paths crossed under the sky,
In every glance, a reason why.
Silent vows, we wander deep,
In this journey, love to keep.

With every step, the story grows,
Through winding roads, our passion flows.
Every twist, a chance to learn,
In the heart, a sacred burn.

Together facing storm and sun,
In each challenge, we're not done.
With trust as our guiding star,
We carry on, no matter how far.

Moments shared, in laughter bright,
Hand in hand, we chase the light.
In every ending, beginnings bloom,
Together we dispel the gloom.

Through valleys low and peaks so high,
Our journeys blend, a sweet reply.
In every heartbeat, love's embrace,
Intertwined paths, sacred space.

The Heart's Silent Oath

In whispers soft, our souls align,
A promise sealed, a bond divine.
Through quiet dreams, our thoughts entwined,
In love's embrace, true peace we find.

With every heartbeat, vows renew,
In depths unseen, our spirits flew.
Through trials faced, we stand as one,
Beneath the stars, our fate begun.

In tender glances, secrets shared,
A silent oath that love has bared.
No words are needed, hearts will speak,
In gentle silence, strong yet meek.

Each dawn that breaks, our love anew,
In golden rays, we chase the blue.
Together bound, through joy and strife,
In every breath, we forge our life.

Through shadows deep, we find our way,
In darkest nights, our hearts won't sway.
The silent vow, forever true,
In every moment, me and you.

Hand in Hand Through Storms

With fingers laced, we face the night,
Through raging winds, we hold on tight.
Each lightning flash, a spark of hope,
Together strong, we learn to cope.

The thunder rolls, yet fear's a friend,
In every storm, our hearts will blend.
With whispered words, we calm the fray,
Hand in hand, we find our way.

As raindrops fall, we laugh and sing,
In tempest's grip, our love takes wing.
The world may shake, but we remain,
In every challenge, love's refrain.

Through swirling skies and darkest hours,
Together we bloom, like vibrant flowers.
In nature's fury, we cast our dreams,
A duo strong, or so it seems.

When after storms, the sun breaks free,
Hand in hand, we cherish glee.
Each moment shared, a precious pearl,
With you, my love, I face the whirl.

A Journey Across Eternity

Through realms unknown, we weave our fate,
In timeless dance, love won't abate.
With every step, a story told,
In secret glances, futures unfold.

Across the stars, our spirits soar,
In every heartbeat, we explore.
The cosmos whispers, guiding light,
In shadows deep, you are my sight.

With open arms, we greet the dawn,
In every sunrise, love reborn.
Through ages passed, we find our way,
Two souls entwined, come what may.

Each path we take, in joy or pain,
In every tear, a sweet refrain.
Across the sands of time we roam,
With you beside me, always home.

In endless skies, our spirits greet,
In every heartbeat, love's heartbeat.
With you, my love, I journey on,
Together forged, forever drawn.

Love's Unyielding Light

In darkest nights, you are my star,
A beacon bright, no matter how far.
Through every shadow, you guide my way,
With love’s pure light, forever stay.

In gentle whispers, warmth unfolds,
A story rich, in silence told.
Each smile shared, a radiant glow,
In love’s embrace, our spirits flow.

When storms arise, and doubts creep in,
Your light shines through, and I begin.
To see the beauty, in every fight,
Together we stand, love's pure delight.

In every challenge, strong we rise,
With hope and grace that never dies.
Through every trial, our hearts ignite,
In love's embrace, unyielding light.

So hand in hand, through life we tread,
With every tear, new dreams we shed.
In love’s embrace, forever bright,
Together we shine, love’s unyielding light.

Roots of Forever

In the earth, we find our place,
Roots entwined in nature's grace.
Holding on through wind and rain,
Whispers of a love unchained.

Branches reaching towards the sky,
A promise that will never die.
From the past, our strength we draw,
Bound together by a law.

Through storms and trials, we will grow,
The bond of roots, a steady flow.
In shadows deep, and sunny light,
Together we will face the night.

When seasons change and colors fade,
In every loss, a memory laid.
The harvest of our hearts we'll share,
With roots that hold beyond compare.

In the silence, gently weave,
The love that only we believe.
Forever intertwined we stand,
In the soil of this shared land.

Timeless Hearts

In the quiet of the night,
Two hearts speak without a sight.
Echoes linger in the dark,
A bond much deeper than a spark.

Threads of time we intertwine,
Moments precious, pure, divine.
In every glance, a silent vow,
For here and now, and even how.

Through the ages, we will roam,
With every heartbeat, coming home.
In laughter shared and tears we shed,
A testament to love widespread.

With every dawn, a new embrace,
Timeless tales we chose to trace.
Through every trial, side by side,
In love's embrace, we always bide.

In the whispers of the stars,
Our journey maps, with no more scars.
Together we will dance and soar,
Timeless hearts forevermore.

Bonds Beyond Time

In the realm where shadows blend,
A bond that knows no page to end.
From every lifetime, we recall,
The threads that weave and never fall.

Past and future intertwine,
We share a bond that's so divine.
In moments lost, we find our way,
A guiding light that will not sway.

Through silence deep, we understand,
The touch of fate's unyielding hand.
In every heartbeat, echoes clear,
A promise held, forever near.

With every journey, new begins,
The web we weave, where love still spins.
With souls aligned, we drift as one,
In every dusk, a rising sun.

Beyond the time, we stand so bold,
In stories yet to be retold.
A testament to what we share,
Bonds beyond time, a love laid bare.

A Dance in Infinity

In the cosmos, we take flight,
Two souls glimmering in the night.
With every step, we spin and sway,
A dance that stretches night and day.

With the stars as our own stage,
We lose ourselves, turn the page.
In the rhythm of the spheres above,
We celebrate this boundless love.

Each twirl a promise made to keep,
In the vastness, love runs deep.
From dusk till dawn, we carve our way,
In the music, forever play.

Through galaxies, hand in hand,
Together we will always stand.
In every heartbeat, whispers sweet,
A dance in time, where worlds meet.

In the silence, let hearts sing,
A timeless bond, eternal spring.
In the echo of the infinite,
Together we will rise, ignite.

Printed in the USA
CPSIA information can be obtained
at www.ICGtesting.com
LVHW020737200924
791511LV00007B/108

9 789916 894583